Why?.
Sometimes there is no why

R Patel and N Hough

Foreword by Kendi Karimi

Copyrights © 2023 R Patel and N Hough

All rights reserved. No part of this book may be reproduced, stored, or transmitted by any means-whether auditory, graphical, mechanical, or electronic-without written permission of the authors. Any unauthorized reproduction of any part of this book is illegal and is punishable by law.

To the maximum extent permitted by law, the authors and publisher disclaim all responsibility and liability to any person, arising directly or indirectly from any person taking or not taking action based on the information available in this publication.

Dedicated to those with unfinished stories of love,

passion, and ambition

Table of Contents

With the grace of the Divine i
Foreword iii
Preface v

HOPE 1
Reflection 3
Reality versus Escapism 4
The Side Effects of Hope 5
My Hope 6
Lost Hope 7
A Letter to Hope 8
Seeds 9
'80s Baby 10
Future 11
Rules 12
Bliss 13
Regrets 14
The End 15
Secrets 16
Evenings 17
Fate 18
Perfection 19
Simplicity 20
Battles 21
Dream State 22
Decisions 23
Conclusion 24

Importance	26
Gamble	27
Moving On	28
Occasions	29
Pretentious	30
Over	31
Happy Pill	32
Immigrant	33
Tea versus Coffee	34
Two-Faced	35
Just One More Day	36
When You Know	37
In-Between	38
Camera	39
Fears	40
Scars	41
Bolt	42
Territorial	43
Every Time	44
Sister	45
2022	46
Free Spirit	48
FAITH	**49**
Faith	51
Holding	52
Emergency	53
#childfreebychoice	54
Baseline	55
Silver Spoon	56

Rudraksha Tree: Elaeocarpus ganitrus	58
Prayer Plant (Maranta leuconeura)	59
Love	60
Safeguarding	61
Cycle of Life	62
How?	63
Evolving	64
Prayers	65
Reset	66
Explore	67
Mistakes	68
Guilt	69
Motherhood	70
Imbalance	71
Infinite	72
Dedication	73
Excel	74
Time	75
Naked	76
Jasmine	77
Teardrops	78
Oneness	79
Parts	80
Bravery	81
Safe Place	82
Failure	83
Coffee	84
Choices	85
Forgiveness	86
Exceptional	87

Appreciation	88
Books	89
Chains	90
Pride	91
Quantity	92
Reflections	93
A Song for Everything	94
Deal Breaker	95
Assistance	96
Fairy Tales	97
Rights	98
Give a Little	99
Space between Prayers	100
Look Back	101
Light	102
25 Percent Discount at a Hotel (True Story)	103
Jeopardise	104
Changes	105
Tired	106
Last Moment	107
Attempt	108
Fear	109
World Peace	110
Forbidden	111
Darkness	112
Unconditional Love	113
Rock Bottom (The Lowest Point of No Return)	114
Animals	115
Faith within Faith	116
Love Yourself First	117

PATIENCE 119
Like Nothing Happened 121
Love at First Sight 122
Unknown 123
Time 124
WTF 125
One 126
Now What? 127
Waiting 128
Losing 129
One Day 130
Unconditional Love 131
It's over 132
Like the Sun and the Moon 133
Plans 134
Sex 135
In-Between 136
Unfinished Business 137
Vulnerability 138
Parents 139
Distance 141
Desperate 142
Choices 143
Impossible 144
Modern Love 145
Rewind 146
Next Time 147
Presence 148
Body Language 149
Living 150

Therapy	151
What If?	152
Motive	153
Space	154
Time Pass	155
Perfect Kiss	156
A Rose	157
Foolish	158
Reputation	159
Lifetime	160
Wake-Up Call	161
Relationships	162
Breaks	163
Paths	164
Opportunities	165
Sleep	166
365	167
Marriage versus Weddings	168
Rest	169
Gold	170
Treachery	171
Convenience	172
Missing	173
To Heal	174
Torture	175
Photographs	176
Identity	177
Call It Quits	178
Coffee Stains	179
One Last Time	180

On the Same Page	181
Worlds Apart	183
Best Bet	184
Strategy	185
Fidelity	186
Forgiveness	187
Partnership	188
Personal Development	189
Body	190
Lifeline	191
Social Events	192
Reasons	193
Shelved	194
Complete the Cycle	195
Merger	196
Blueprint	197
Value	198
Discover	199
Refine	200
Patience within Patience	201
One More, Just One More!	202
Destruction	203
Time	204
Mind	205
With Patience	206
Why?	207
He Who Asks Receives	208
Purpose	210
Authors	211

With the grace of the Divine

HOPE, FAITH, and PATIENCE—they are the three most vital ingredients for survival. They are as important as earth, water, air, and fire—the key elements of life.

This book, therefore, is divided into three chapters reflecting emotions, struggles, and achievements in life that some will be able to resonate with.

Foreword

Oftentimes, you find yourself asking the question: Why? "Why did this happen to me? Why hasn't this happened for me? Why didn't I have more time?" There are so many versions of why. And when there is no answer from the other side, you find that you have to dig up some internal strength to continue on with life. You have to trust it when things are hard and when they are easy. Maybe the answer to why lies in the act of our courage. In the proof of our survival despite it all.

This book does not try to answer your why. It gives you an insight into the "how" of life, the reasons behind your tears and your smiles. It gives you insight into hope and love, with love. It shows you how to plant your seeds and let them grow. It holds your hand amid the many confusing questions of life and says to you, "Me too." Why? Because sometimes there is no why, there's just a way to get through. I felt understood after reading this book. It's not the kind of book that you read just once. Spread the word.

Kendi Karimi
Author and businesswoman

Preface

This book takes you on a journey of self-discovery, hope, heartbreak, joy, tears, and self-doubt to self-love. You feel all the emotions that the authors have gone through and it helps the reader to process the emotions they have felt through their own journey.

Nidhi Rupa Joshi

Author of *Fireflies and Shooting Stars* series of books, podcast host, NLP coach and speaker (UK)

This timely and inspiring collection of observations invites reflection and contemplation at a particularly challenging period for people across the globe. It encompasses a range of themes and emotions that will resonate with anyone who has ever loved, lost, laughed, cried, or hoped. I found myself feeling melancholy, amused, tearful, joyful, and ultimately hopeful.

Mindful writing such as this warrants repeat readings and I look forward to revisiting and reflecting on many of the observations included in this text. I highly recommend this book, which does not attempt to answer the "why" questions in life but rather the "how" questions, which shines a light on the processes that define "who we are" as individuals struggling to make sense of the increasingly complex world, we live in.

Atoosa Sepehr

Writer and photographer (UK)

HOPE

Reflection

When you stumbled into my life you stabilised me. When you walked out, I stumbled like never before. Questioning myself, "But why?" Sure, you rocked my world, sweetheart, but you also turned it upside down.

What I should have asked was, "Why did I stumble?" rather than asking myself, "Why did you leave?" It made me question the three pillars of life that I firmly believed in: Hope. Faith. Patience.

Reality versus Escapism

You can only hope that the next person you meet is not a filmmaker or a script where you don't need to use the following terms and words:

1. Ghosting
2. Narcissistic
3. Liar
4. Broken

The Side Effects of Hope

"Anything that gives you hope, surely that's a good thing, right?"

Even if it's a false hope, surely the human body will respond the same? If not, then with the side effects of hope, maybe one can benefit from the placebo effects of hope.

My Hope

My every hope begins and ends with you. My every hopelessness begins and ends with you. Even if it's the hope of the unexpected.

Lost Hope

Whenever you feel like a broken heart has left you in pain and you have lost all hope, see a cardiologist and ask for the true definition of a "broken heart." Seek gratitude for your beating heart, and you will find hope again.

A Letter to Hope

First, I would like to thank you for accompanying me over the years with your presence. You gave me strength and consoled me when I needed it the most. You always reassured me that my love was very much real.

However, I need you to leave me now. Until I have you by my side, it will be impossible for me to move on, to see sense, to get closure and move on. Until I have you, I will continue to wait for something that might never happen, always and forever.

So, you see, hope, as much as I want you to stay with me, what I need is for you to leave me now. The one I love is never returning.

Please do come back to me when I have the capability to hold on to you and hope for a miracle that will never happen. Unless, of course, you know something that I don't.

Seeds

The seed of hope once planted is "evergreen" and everlasting. Nothing, not even facts, evidence, and information that hold up, can uproot it. Over the years, it only gets stronger. So let it be, let it grow, let it find its way. So that one day, it can guide you.

'80s Baby

*B*orn in the '80s, grew up in the '90s. A fusion of Disney and Bollywood movies. Chances are you will always hope for a "movie-like happy ending?" This can either draw one to positivity with hope or towards darkness with disappointment.

Future

We all do things to the best of our ability and capacity. In the hope that our next generation won't repeat the same mistakes we made. Break the pattern of our past generations and ours.

I only hope they will love more wisely.

Rules

Before falling in love, there should be a rule book. A book that teaches you how to "fall out of love" first before falling in love. Just like knowing the exit routes before entering an unknown area.

It sure as hell would save a lot of time and effort now, wouldn't it? At least you live in the moment rather than living in one's memories.

Bliss

To be the architect of your own life

    To tailor your career to your life

    To make life choices to suit your living

    This can only be achieved with faith.

Faith to know that it is okay to listen to your heart and go where your soul takes you. Faith that it is okay to follow your passion, where your calling is.

Faith that even if your lineage ends with you, you have planted the seed to carry on your legacy to change the world for the better.

Regrets

When we never thought that far down the line, and now, no amount of reflection can soften the blow. Things we did out of foolishness, stupidity, or at times, without even a reason.

The End

Just as I believe it is over, you give me hope.

Just as I think my prayers have bounced back, you ask me to hold on to that faith.

Just as I feel like giving up, you tell me to have patience.

But, darling, I can't hold on to hope, faith, and patience for the both of us anymore. Everyone has an end point, and I have reached mine.

Secrets

𝒶 person's biggest weakness . . . greater than love.
Nothing more, nothing less.

Evenings

It comes empty-handed and leaves empty-handed. And with every evening that passes without your return, it dries up another reserve of tears.

Give it another few years and there will be nothing else to come home to.

Fate

I can't pray for you to come back into my life; it wouldn't be fair.

I can't ask you to leave your life for me since I lost that right when you left in the first place.

I can only hope that maybe one day the stars will align and the dots will join backwards.

Perfection

We were perfect together, but clearly, you saw the perfection in our separation.

Simplicity

If only it were that simple.

Battles

Some battles just weren't worth fighting for. Yet those are the ones we seem to regret for the rest of our lives—not fighting.

Dream State

If missing you in reality wasn't bad enough, now I miss you in my dreams too.

Decisions

The worst decision one can make is a decision that eliminates a later.

Therefore, if there is a possible "later," there will always be hope.

Conclusion

You appeared before me that day, and from that one meeting, I concluded you were the one, without any evidence other than a gut feeling or investment of time from you.

I should have checked for the facts and information that would hold up and found a primary end point, as if it was like a clinical trial. It would have saved a tragedy.

A tragedy one may never get over. Yet, I have gratitude that within this tragedy, I found myself.

Enough

You love me.
    I love you.
    God's our witness.
    I thought that was enough, didn't you?

Importance

I want my importance to be in your heart as yours is in mine.

Titles and entitlements have their limitations and so their significance does not matter to me.

Gamble

You were my biggest gamble, my biggest risk in life.

Every play, every bet was with that little hope that fate may show some mercy and grace.

Losing my everything . . . pride, wealth, possessions, and mind.

. . . Just to win back your love that somehow slipped away from me in silence, even when the chance of winning you back was negligible.

I should have stopped whilst I was ahead, should have stopped when I saw the first sign of losing. Never should I have gambled all my time away.

Moving On

No matter how many branches a tree grows, its existence is in its trunk and roots. It can't move. That is how it feels when someone tells me to "move on!" If I move on from you, my love, it will wipe out my existence and destroy me.

Occasions

Buy rescue plants in times of sadness or plant seedlings.

Share your sadness with it, and it will provide the comfort, hope, and faith you need.

Buy a blossomed plant in times of joy to mark a moment or a new season.

It will remind you of the significance of humility, gratitude, and patience.

This way, every plant you invest in will have a story. Your story requires no words or lyrics. Your senses will be enough to experience it. Your garden will be your unique selling proposition.

Pretentious

You looked so happy. You looked so elated. You looked so full of life

Yet your eyes searched for peace, contentment, and passion like never before.

Over

You always know.

    Always.

    Yet you always seem to find an excuse to have hope that it isn't over.

    Always.

Happy Pill

If you were a pill, I'd want a lifelong prescription.
 If only you weren't like a restricted, "controlled drug."

Immigrant

Born to parents of immigrants, yet at times, rather than being the fabric of the nation, you still feel a subtle hint, a civilised and unspoken form of racism at each step of progression. I pray the pattern breaks for the next generation to come together, having the freedom of not being judged by race, clan, class, colour, or birthright but by one's merit, ability, and competence.

Tea versus Coffee

Since when did a relationship ever start with tea?

Unless it is a "chai" perhaps, something sexy, sensual, and comforting about it. Like an arranged marriage, which usually starts off with a "chai."

Rather than a love marriage, where "it all started with a coffee."

Two-Faced

Aren't we all? Some more than others.

So how can we expect others to not ever be two-faced towards us?

There are no bad people, but some just have more goodness in them than others.

Just One More Day

I'll give it twenty-four hours.

I manage to give a valid reason to extend the expiration date every night.

I justify the extension to cut you off, to accept, and set a deadline to move on.

Maybe the root cause is an unconscious bias of an emotional construct, allowing me to think it's acceptable to not use my God-given intelligence?

And waste my days away.

If you didn't give me a choice and set the deadline for me, would I follow it through?

When You Know

All the facts, information, and evidence hold up.

Yet every part of me, if I were the jury, finds you "not guilty."

Do me a favour, my dear. Just plead "not guilty."

In-Between

I wish I could build a wall between you and me. A wall made of air.

Air unpolluted and space so divine and cosmic.

Separated yet breathing the same space.

Camera

I can only hold on to memories we made unless I'm screwed over with dementia.

Hence, I'm in love with my camera to capture my past, present, and the seed for the future. I photograph the journey of life, the body, which is the transportation of my soul and reflection of my mind.

Fears

I can only face one fear at a time now.

    Unless someone can transform my multiple fears, anxiety, and phobias into music by which I can find a way out. And come through fearless.

Scars

If only unseen and unspoken scars were acknowledged the same as those seen. Not by outsiders but by your own.

Bolt

Your every word

    Your every promise

    Strikes me like a bolt of lightning when broken, every single time. Each time, the current is amplified. I can only pray for the rainbow to appear in time before it is too late to find the silver lining.

Territorial

You marked your territory not with kisses but with scars on my soul and memories that I can't wipe away. You left no space for another to replace you within my heart.

Every Time

Every time I come home, you greet me with such joy
    Holding always out to me,
    your very favourite toy
    Every time I have to leave
    you try your hardest to follow me
    out of the door
    Or cry or whine, not to be, without me, which
upsets me even more

    I miss you every minute of every day now that you are gone, no longer by my side
    You guarded me, loved me unconditionally emotionally, and helped me through the days before you died.
    My heart hurts and I want you to know that the unconditional deep love you gave to me will never be forgotten
    My heart longs to be with you once more. I have never felt so low.
    My heart sits deep in my chest, torn in two feelings, like it's taken the greatest blow.

Sister

You were strong and full of hope and faith that the miracle of wellness would come.

You loved life and wanted more time in this world to spend more time with those you loved to get more done.

You just had come to terms with an end-of-life diagnosis and so put in place your full bucket list of most "do" experiences before you died, as you always said that life was a cycle and you were along for the ride.

THEN a pandemic called Covid hit the world at full scale; death was all around and ever nearer. But you still had hope and faith to fight the fight and carry on. There was nothing clearer.

You tried so hard to complete your bucket list, but it became a distant memory; life and your world suddenly became very small for you. But you chose to do what you could do. And look at the situation as just temporary.

When asked if you were scared of dying, you replied, "No, I have faith," and started crying.

Goodbye for now. We will meet again, for when my time comes, I will follow the light . . . and there you'll be in clear sight.

2022

A war thought never to come forth
Cultural heritage being destroyed
Shifting regions, shifting borders
Human displacement, world famine
Global living, financial and climate crises

The Western world, powerful politicians, the bedrock of peace
Thought to be a secure democracy
No commitment
Struggling and juggling
Men, women, children, mankind
Suffering but still enduring

Young men torn from their families to fight with all their might
Women and children flee
Not knowing what will be
An independent country
Once full of life, now full of strife
Once a vision, now division
Once full of light now a dark sight

"Will we still be alive to see another day?" When will peace arrive?

Hope! Hope! Have faith that your home and country will and must survive.

Free Spirit

Free spirits (individual energy aura and causes that are expressed with or without universal constraints)

Community spirit (groups of individuals that come together forming a very powerful energy, aura, and cause, often for the greater good, with or without universal constraints)

FAITH

Faith

Incredible, isn't it? What faith can do to our expectations?

It makes you believe in the unexpected. If you hold on to it long enough, miracles might just happen.

Holding

*H*olding on to faith is like holding on to your soul in more ways than one. If only there was a protocol to follow on how to do this, without reading the entire never-ending goddamn policy.

Emergency

Faith has been the saving grace, like a defibrillator to the cardiac arrest that I had when you left.

However, the fact that you are not returning stopped the heart a second time.

How many more times can there be a successful resuscitation, when each time, every cell is deprived of oxygen, reducing its need each time? It is as if the hope diminishes with each recurrence.

I can't imagine what would happen if faith doesn't get there in time.

#childfreebychoice

"Yes, it is okay to be child-free by choice. And don't let anyone tell you any different." This is what my mind, body, and soul said with total faith.

Baseline

When you start from nothing, you have to build your own foundation, even if you crumble to your knees. You never fear rebuilding again and again since you already have the tools and know-how to rebuild, improvise, be stronger and even more beautiful than ever before.

More importantly, it's yours to build whatever you want; it will hold anything. So, have faith in the foundation that you built alone. It will always be stronger than others.

Silver Spoon

Some people are born with privileges, some are born with opportunities.

Some people are born fortunate, and some people are just born blessed.

However, how would you define privileges, opportunities, good fortune, and blessings? Or is it how content you are, how much validation you need, health, wealth, or intelligence?

Or is it how close your soul is to inner peace?

Belief

Even if you don't believe in God, have faith. Faith alone will carry you.

Rudraksha Tree:
Elaeocarpus ganitrus

An evergreen tree.

They say it is meant to absorb negative energy and radiate positive energy. I hope so. Since I've told it all my secrets, worries, and sadness. Therefore, I believe it must be true. Otherwise, how can else can I explain its survival and mine too.

Prayer Plant (Maranta leuconeura)

Today I learnt of a very special plant called a "prayer plant." Such a beautiful name for a plant, isn't it?

A perfect name to reflect its nature.

At night, it closes its leaves, and at dawn, opens up again.

How many of us have actually had the patience to watch this process?

Maybe our prayers are always answered, but we just might not be awake at the right time to receive the answer. Possible, isn't it?

Love

Who really knows? As long as you know what it means to you. Surely, that is all that matters.

Safeguarding

Sometimes, in order to safeguard others, we forget to guard ourselves.

Then finally, when we do make the effort, we make a heartfelt wish for divine intervention. The protection cast over is just impossible to pierce through. As if it was protection made to perfection.

Cycle of Life

There is just one.

How?

"How do you know?" asked the mind.
"You just do!" said the heart.

Evolving

Being in love with you was the most beautiful enigma of my life. However, I evolved in our separation.

Prayers

It is what gets us through life when all else fails.

Reset

Somehow, an unseen, unexplained force just comes, shocking you to your core, only to shut you down and reset. Never be afraid to restart this way.

Explore

How do you know that there isn't anything out there unless you have the courage? The courage to walk the path of the unknown, where one has never been.

So go out there. I promise you there is a light beyond the dark cave you think you are in. You have seen and experienced the darkness at its best. Now go, my child, and embrace the light at its best. Go experience and appreciate the spirit of life. Faith alone will guide you. I promise.

Mistakes

Sometimes we make decisions to protect the heart, soul, and reputation even. Knowing full well it might be a mistake.

Perhaps it is because it was the only mistake we were willing to make at the time. However, was it really a mistake? If given a second chance, would we still do the same thing?

Guilt

A very wise friend told me once, "Guilt is a useless emotion. You can't do anything with it." How right she was.

Motherhood

Can also be "PAWsitive."

Imbalance

I didn't know how to maintain balance until faith taught me how to get the perfect equilibrium.

Had you not caught me off-guard, I would never have understood this secret.

Infinite

Souls made of wood walk into the sea and return being able to explain the experience.

Souls made of salt walk into the sea and are unable to return to explain the experience; they just dissolve into the ocean.

Maybe that's the difference between making love and being in love?

Once you fall in love with that one soul, there is no point of return.

Dedication

I don't know if it's faith or determination that is keeping me dedicated to you.

Loving you is like a prayer in itself.

The difference is that sometimes it feels like praying in hope and sometimes it feels like praying in faith. Loving you is easy, but loving you patiently is the hardest thing that I have ever had to do.

Excel

Music written for entertainment compared to music made for devotion will always excel. Listen out for the difference next time.

Time

As time goes on, it takes away your chances of fulfilling your dreams, ambitions, and desires. We all get an annual reminder of that, highlighting our unfinished life plans.

However, in meditation, we reflect. In prayer, we see gratitude. In light, we realise how far we have actually come. The success, the opportunities, the achievements, and life experiences we loved more than others are mostly due to unplanned events.

Sometimes we forget that the amazing calibre of talent can be found through the least expected. Moral of the story:

1. Plan your life to your soul's desire for contentment.
2. Never plan to everyone else's standards or you will always have limitations in your mind, body, and spirit.
3. Use your intellect to find a higher cause and a bigger vision.
4. Question everything without fear.

Naked

Strip away your qualifications and certificates.
Strip away your assets and wealth.
Then see who remains in your life.

Jasmine

Most people love it for its scent and beauty.

I love it for its character.

You can cut it right down to its roots, and it will still grow upwards and onwards, resilient to every season. The sun may burn it, but provided its roots are intact with the grace of Mother Nature, it will always re-establish itself.

Considering it's such a delicate-looking plant, its character is in its strength.

So, plant not one but many in your life or at least surround yourself in its aura. If nothing else for the reminders it gives you.

Teardrops

Tears of joy or sadness, they are alike in theory.

In practice, every drop has its own story, its own meaning, its own value, and its own moment.

Sometimes, you can't explain the depth of your tears to anyone other than the Divine.

Oneness

It is a lot harder not to hate anyone compared to loving all. There is a difference. When humanity learns the art of not hating anyone, that is when I believe we will see heaven on earth.

Parts

A part of me will always belong to you. And a part of you will always belong to me. Period.

Bravery

I pray for bravery over you any day. Being brave is what carried me in life. When I met you, I thought maybe I didn't need to be so brave anymore.

Having you by my side, I knew I could face anything.

Little did I know, dealing with a heart broken by you required me to be the bravest in my life. It was the first time in my life I tasted disappointment. Therefore, I pray never to forget "the art of bravery."

Safe Place

In the presence of the Divine, be that at a place of worship or any place of tranquillity.

Nowadays, I can't share that space with others who are not on the same wavelength. I can't understand why others can't appreciate the moment, the opportunity, to connect to a higher being in silence.

Small talk fills the space with useless trivia. Activities of daily living take over, like a playground or school pickups. Conversations with God dilute in mindless conversations, losing the essence of mindfulness.

Failure

It happens to the best of us.

    Prepare again

    Practice again

    Pray again.

As long as there is life, there will always be another chance.

Keep trying at every God-given opportunity with faith. Never give up, if the intention is there, if the heart is in the right place, if the cause is selfless. Trust me, you will be grateful for the lessons that the failures taught you.

There is great pleasure in labour when that labour is for a higher cause and in aid of others.

Respect those that were critical of you as there are lessons there too.

Coffee

Like relationships, coffee is best accompanied by purified water. Even when it is cold, it never loses its essence or taste.

Choices

Between righteousness and love, what do you choose? Pray and listen to your soul, I say.

Forgiveness

Sometimes, the hardest thing to do is forgive yourself. What is even harder is to forgive oneself for actions one didn't even know were wrong at the time, even if they were corrected over time.

However, one has to pick a time and just let go.

Remember, those mistakes too were a part of life, a part of fate, a part of destiny, and a part of learning.

That is what being human is all about, isn't it? Or else, we would all be an epiphany of perfection. And there would be nothing to reflect, revive, and rejuvenate. Nor would there be new learnings, new lessons, and new experiences for the future generation to learn from.

Exceptional

... *B*ecome the perfect student by allowing the mentor to pick you. Trust your mentor with total dedication and devotion.

Never set limitations to your mindset. Only then will you expose yourself to unlimited resources, knowledge, skills, and wisdom. This is what will make you excel and stand apart from others. And that is what will attract extraordinary mentors towards you at every step, throughout your life.

Appreciation

I pray that in my neighbourhood every house has a magical looking garden and a beautiful front yard with a twinkle of lights in the evening. So that my walks are full of inspiration, beauty, motivation, and a reminder of God's miracles on earth.

Books

Always respect a book. It will either teach you what to do or what not to do to protect yourself.

Chains

Sometimes we get enchained within our own self-made chains, and unless these are broken in time, we wear them like an ornament instead of breaking free from them.

Sometimes we make them out of paper, as we did in childhood, and over time, we forget how easy it is to break free from them in adulthood.

Pride

Keep the path of righteousness and the truth in your heart, soul, and actions.

And you will never lose your glory and honour.

Seek guidance in prayers, as sometimes, the simplest logic may feel like the most complicated route to follow.

Quantity

I have never measured my love for you in the distance we had nor the years between us but in the depth of our love.

Reflections

Daily reminders to pray with faith.

Daily reminders to have patience with hope.

The only way to reflect, to grow, to forgive, and to love.

Keep banking the reflections in numbers towards light, for in life, the "devil" may draw you towards the darkness.

Reflections done in good faith will never lose their luminance. Trust the divine that lives within your soul.

A Song for Everything

Have a morning song. Have an evening song

Have a song of the day, of the week, of the month, of the year, of the decade

Have a song to mark both the joy and grief

Even music without any lyrics will do magic if you just allow it to

Just pick what your soul is drawn to rather than what your ears are tuned to.

Deal Breaker

At what point do you leave the table?

At what point do you call it quits?

At what point do you say "enough"?

At what point do you stop asking "why"?

I guess it's the point when you have more confidence within yourself and the Divine than whomever it is that you are waiting for to change or return. Isn't it?

Assistance

Do I burn all of your recollections and reminiscences into aches?

    Do I drown our past in the ocean?

    Do I take our time to the crematorium to be buried deep into the ground?

    Do I hand over your thoughts to the wind?

    Oh, for God's sake, which element do I request to give me the boon to disconnect from you?

Fairy Tales

Why aim to be a princess when you can aim to be the queen, that too the queen of hearts?

Rights

Who has the right over time? So, just have faith in the generosity of time given by life itself. No one can take that away from you. That is your right.

Give a Little

Drop by drop, you give when expected, not realising that you are at the point of dehydration. So, sometimes, the best gift you can give someone is the "gift of NO."

Space between Prayers

Take comfort that even if you don't pray, the Divine will still know the depth of your tears.

Take comfort that even if you don't show attendance at a place of worship, your soul will still be acknowledged.

Sometimes we need to take a step back and reflect on what we are actually praying for.

Sometimes it may be taking a break. A break by not praying at all. Take time out. This doesn't mean you give up and lose faith.

It just means, sometimes it's like people renewing their vows. We may need space to renew what we are praying for.

Look Back

My best friend tells me every year, when I am about to turn a year older and feel I haven't achieved all I wanted till then:

"Look back at your old eighteen-year-old self. Would she have believed you if you told her you will achieve what you have achieved to date?"

Sometimes you need to look back rather than look ahead. The past too is also the grace of life in which we find gratitude. Patience has no use if you give up before you succeed, desire has no use if you have no goals, and thoughts have no use if you don't take a step or a risk to action it.

Light

Some people light a candle for light and warmth. And then there are some people that just spread radiance in their presence independent of anything.

Aim to radiate or stay in the presence of radiance.

25 Percent Discount at a Hotel (True Story)

Me: So, you added the 25 percent discount on the breakfast?

Waiter: No ma'am, the discount is applied only after midnight.

Me: Why? Because the cost of the tomatoes and mushrooms goes up by 25 percent after midnight?

Some laughs are worth paying the extra 25 percent for.

Jeopardise

Fully aware of what I am losing, what I am missing out on, and what disadvantage I am at.

Impossible to find hope, yet I have faith in a divine solution to find myself and take me out of this dilemma.

Changes

Sometimes I think that

> I would have flourished in my own element without you.
>
> Then reflect and realise that your sorrow and pain fuelled my determination.
>
> Hence, you had a significant contribution towards my transformation and success.

Tired

My last painful cry was over you.

My last real laugh was with you.

I tried to seek a greater pain to get over it and tried to find a greater joy than you.

Failed attempts are all I achieve. And therefore, I pray for grace to fall upon me and put a hand over me and tell me, "Enough now, child. Stop trying and let it be."

Last Moment

Faith is the safety net.
  Hope is the lifeline.
  No matter what happens, never lose patience, for it's the fine line between belief and a miracle waiting to happen.

Attempt

Try, and you may become stronger.

However, not trying is a guaranteed way of weakening your soul, either by living in regret of not trying or disabling yourself just because you "think" you can't.

Fear

The root of all injustice and the road to bitterness.

Take a step with a prayer to speak out against injustice, no matter how small.

Don't think the silence will exempt you from being affected.

One drop of joy, and the experience is felt in all its surroundings and is contagious. So does a drop of sorrow that contaminates its surroundings.

For this reason, shape and form your clouds wisely without fear. You never know when you will need them to drizzle or cause a storm.

World Peace

In summary, it means:

a) Compassion
b) Righteousness
c) Sacrifice

. . . towards society and planet earth under a duty of care by every single soul.

Forbidden

We try to pray to live by a righteous path in life, right?

Yet at times you have the devil, not just to encourage you, but guiding the way. That's the point at which you pray your hardest; that your hopes and patience do not break.

Darkness

Be it inner or outer darkness, prayers give hope that illuminate like nothing else. If you don't believe in prayers, hold on to your duty towards your responsibilities in life. Follow the path of duty sincerely, and the path will light up for you. In summary, do your "karma" with a higher ideal and a higher spirit will guide you.

Unconditional Love

Unconditional love does exist but is entwined with the need and want to silently protect, often existing between your child or children, and often, animal companions.

Rock Bottom (The Lowest Point of No Return)

*E*xhausted and confused, numb and isolated a nothingness, a nowhere, a HOLE, a BLACK HOLE.

> A falling, not knowing where or what you're falling from Survival instincts far gone.
>
> No one or nothing, just that person at rock bottom, can make them get up and carry on.
>
> When it becomes unbearable that's when the light comes on, or it is done.
>
> Get up, get over it, is often said, but those words are misleading.
>
> The kindness, strength, and support of others can have a positive effect Help to get up and start again crawling slowly out of the dread.
>
> The earth that is sown
>
> The regrowth of the soul, the touch of the soil, and the feelings of attachment are grown again.
>
> Trust me, I KNOW!

Animals

Animals are healers and do miracles for mental health. Their unconditional love and the difference they make is irrefutable—their need to care for you. They expect nothing of you and still give everything in return. They give you a purpose to live, and that's essential. That's what got me up.

Faith within Faith

𝓑e told in a strong belief of any religion Often based on a spiritual conviction

    An optimism in expectations and hopefulness A reliance, a credence, a willingness.
        A trust or a confidence in someone or something
        Giving rise to optimism with dependence forming.

A hope for the best outcome
A prayer to the heavens
Sometimes a desperation
That calls for amens

A quiet resolution for only you to know
The seed of faith sown, ready to grow
A flower so beautiful in full bloom
A message to a bride and groom
Faith is all and everything
A hand on the heart in good times and bad
In happy times and around for the sad Faith is all and everything.

Love Yourself First

Why do I love you ? I ask myself
    Is it your looks, personality, or wealth?
    Is it because you make me laugh so?
    Or is it because you encourage me to grow?

    Why do you love me? I always wonder
    As my mood swings are like sunshine and thunder
    Is it because I let you be who you are
    Standing there, drinking beer at the bar?

    Whatever a marriage should really be
    We are together, and that's what matters to me.
    Through the good, the bad, the laughs, and the struggles
    It's well worth it for all the love and cuddles.

    Never be someone different from who you truly are
    As it's like putting on a different face and changing your persona
    From self-awareness comes confidence
    In turn learning to have strong resilience.

PATIENCE

Like Nothing Happened

You walked back into my life, and it was as if you never left.
Like your separation happened another lifetime ago.

Love at First Sight

The first sight. Oh, my, the first time we met. How is it that to see you again, after what feels like a whole lifetime, still feels like the first time?

Who knew what a beautiful gamble this would be?

Unknown

Unknown to you, but because of you, I learnt the definition of patience. It is a fine art to master this skill too.

Time

Who knows if time can ever heal the trauma caused by false hope? Who knows if we carry this hope into another life? Maybe to save everybody's time, "hope" should have an expiry date?

WTF

Whatever did I hope for? Whatever did you hope for? What the hell were we thinking?

Did we start something that shouldn't have ended, or did we end something before it even started?

In the hope of what?

One

Many can touch our lives and not make a difference. Then there is that one.

Now What?

You came back into my life as if you never left.

Now you have left again, as if you never even came back in the first place.

Do I live in the hope, with faith or patience for your return?

Waiting

I wait with hope
I wait with faith
Now, the above is possible, but how the f*ck do I wait with patience?

Losing

I have lost you many times in one lifetime that I think I have developed immunity to your absence.

One Day

When you start thinking . . .

One day I will meet my soul mate
One day I will fall in love again
One day I will meet the one
One day I will find my life partner
And then you think . . .
"Oh f*ck! What if that one day never comes?"

Hence, the importance of another passion, another reason to love, another vision, another reason to live like it's your last day . . . because, my darling, independence and the freedom to live with health are priceless gifts.

Unconditional Love

Just accept it. It doesn't exist in human relationships. How else can you explain disappointment?

It's over

"Get over it!" said none that loved and lost

Like the Sun and the Moon

My love for you is like the sun—there every day, without fail, it rises and sets like clockwork, and you see it every day as it is, whole. It distributes its energy eventually on the earth and is predictable.

Your love for me is like the moon—you see it whole once a month; otherwise, you see it in sections, including nights of total eclipse.

Plans

"It wasn't meant to be this way . . . this was so not the plan!" Yet, we forget that some unplanned events have given us the best outcomes to perfection that no amount of planning could do.

Sex

It is what it is.

Yet, if you do your research, each century comes with its own definition based on its needs for survival and convenience.

In-Between

That place when it isn't just sex but not quite love—an unspoken and indescribable connection. Not quite living in reality and not quite on cloud nine. Not in the real world and not quite past the other side.

Unfinished Business

As long as there is you and as long as there is me, it wouldn't matter how far apart we are.

"It" will never be off the table.

Vulnerability

You knew me before I was strong, you understood my weaknesses before they became my strengths.

I knew you before you were weak, I understood your strengths before they became your weaknesses.

I wonder what a combination we would make now.

Parents

They do things to the best of their ability and capacity.

You realise this as you see them age with you as you mature in life.

However, you will never catch up with them. So, choose your time wisely.

A Breakup

*N*othing but an introduction to the "Kübler-Ross GRIEF CYCLE."

Distance

When we both can't see the sun or the moon and the stars at the same time.

Desperate

For you, my love, always. My mind, body, and soul.

Choices

Do we really have a choice in whom we fall in love with?

If that's true, then surely, we would have the luxury of choosing to fall out of love with someone, isn't it?

Impossible

Can't escape it.
    Can't unsee it.
    Can't unhear it.
    Can't undo it.
    That one momentary slip was, without doubt, worth a lifetime of waiting.

Modern Love

I'm quite certain it was a lot harder to fall in love before the advent of the smartphone and social media, yet somehow a lot easier to get over someone.

Rewind

When you feel like the heartache is too much and beyond repair. When the pain seems so excruciating.

Rewind back to the moments of your life when things seemed impossible to get through. Hardships that just seemed like there was no end to and situations you had no control over.

Somehow, grace or a kindred spirit managed to pull you out of it, isn't it? And somehow, those unfortunate events managed to enhance your life in ways that even fortunate events wouldn't have done.

How it summarises your whole life's heartache versus one broken relationship that bruised your heart and soul.

Hopefully, you will realise that as real as the pain is, life's burden will always be greater. So, if you can get through to life, you will get through this also. This too will pass, only for you to rewind it back to one.

Next Time

So, it didn't work out. Another lifetime maybe. I will live with that desire "alone" but will never compromise or accept a consolation prize.

Presence

... And here we are.

How can you restrict thoughts? At least with a moral compass, you can at least control one's actions. I can only pray that when we are in each other's presence at least one of our compasses is in working order.

Body Language

You know it, and I know it.

A language of its own shared between us. To translate it without losing its essence is an art in itself.

Living

Until there is a heartbeat.
   Until there is a breath.
   Until there is a spirit of love, hope, and faith.

Therapy

Like having a declutter of your history.

To archive the parts, to put things behind, and compartmentalise to make way for a new perspective.

Re-prioritise for clarity.

Making way for new learning, new beginnings, new opportunities, new experiences, another love, another passion for life.

What If?

There will always be a "what if" between us. Now and forever.

Motive

Whatever the motive was, you should have said it from the start. Just like how you articulated so beautifully and clearly when you told me you loved me.

Space

You needed space. But I needed an explanation. Together, we needed closure. How unfortunate is it that you realised now.

Time Pass

Everything, everyone, every experience and every relationship will always be in passing.

At least until your return or no return.

Perfect Kiss

There will always be a benchmark where passion, love, lust, intimacy, and spirit combine.

A Rose

I'm that rose you won't find at a florist. Well preserved, without any thorns risking an injury. Nor the rose you would find in a flower arrangement, not even at a garden exhibition.

However, you will find me in the wild, free.

As a climbing rose with its thorns.

So, don't try to pick me, don't try to hold me nor come close.

Build a beautiful fence and have patience. Just remember, I'm a climbing rose; I will go against gravity. So don't try to tame me and don't force me in a direction against my nature and free spirit.

Foolish

Falling in love can be foolish. Unable to fall out of love is even worse!

Reputation

It's nothing but a collection of opinions made of different value systems.

Being objective rather than subjective matters the most.

Lifetime

All children want is our time, and all parents want, in their old age, is our time.

We often don't realise the value of time in adolescence and adulthood.

However, blessed are those that realise we don't have forever in middle age to make amends and make up for the lost time.

If ever you need to make a decision in adolescence or in adulthood where you have two choices, just think, "Is there a chance I may reject it when I am forty years old?" Then make that call.

If ever you are in doubt about making amends in adolescence or in adulthood, just think, "Is this where I really want the relationship to be when I am forty years old?" Then see if you still have any doubts.

Wake-Up Call

Sometimes it takes a wake-up call to realise that one has to slow down.

Otherwise, the mind or the body will do it for you, and it might not be at your convenience.

Therefore, use you mind, body, and intellect to stop, reassess, and recoup.

Embrace the wake-up call of being grateful for its timing, have faith that it is never too late.

Just remember, changing a lifetime of habits for a different outcome will not change in days, weeks, months, or even years. However, have patience, because things will change as change is evitable.

Take it back to basics.

One step at a time.

One change at a time.

One wake-up call at a time, or there will be many in life.

Relationships

In relationships, we seek complete satisfaction, security, and happiness at every stage. Yet relationships are the root cause of our greatest griefs too, or is it expectations from the relationships?

Breaks

Whenever you think life is breaking you down.

Stop, reflect, pray. It might be that life is trying to give you a break. So, take a break, rest, recoup, and heal.

Take as long as you need and have faith that even though you are walking the road for a long time, you won't break down.

Paths

The universe has its ways, so trust its powers. It will create a path for you. Just make a start and make a list of goals, assigning an action plan for each goal.

Trust the divine grace of the universe to help you make a start. Aim for a path not just for your own gain but one where others can progress, prosper, and be inspired too.

Pray you learn the difference between being alone and loneliness so that you realise your capabilities and have the confidence, by always seeking knowledge along the way.

Each generation has its own journey. Hence, possibly, the new generation may not be successful and happy with the same path. So don't set traditions and rules that are not flexible.

Opportunities

New problems and challenges will keep coming, but remember, the solutions will always be within the problems.

Give yourself a chance and the time to be inquisitive, to explore and find a solution.

Don't waste time in the wonderment of why, what, when, and how.

Sleep

What used to be one of the most simple and natural things to people is now either a skill one has to learn or a blessing.

365

Each day that passes without you is as good as 365 days rolled into one.

Yet each day with you is like 365 seconds rolled into one.

Marriage versus Weddings

Of course, there is a difference between a beautiful marriage and a beautiful wedding.

Blessed are those that have both.

Privileged are those that don't need a wedding but have a relationship above and beyond the definition of a marriage.

Rest

When the mind runs a marathon, the body never gets any rest, even in the middle of all the comforts and luxuries in attendance.

In slow motion, you can identify a pattern and errors, allowing you to make corrections. Otherwise, you will never change the outcome.

Gold

Once recreated by an expert goldsmith, it loses its monetary value but gains its value in beauty and appearance.

Hence, isn't it better to let it stay in its raw, compressed form, where the value is greater in weight rather than in the hands of an amateur?

So, either create your own worth solo or have the patience to wait for the right soul to enhance your value.

Treachery

When you break a promise
    When you don't keep your word
    When you don't give an explanation
    When you use avoidance
    When you give false hope
    When you can't call it betrayal or infidelity, yet it feels the same.

Convenience

A safety net of three:

1. Don't fall in love
2. Know each other's boundaries
3. Friends with benefits

Missing

If I could, I would report a missing soul. However, I don't possess any evidence to prove that you belong to me. However, somehow, if I ever went missing, you have everything you need to show that I belonged and still belong to you . . . Because I never belonged to anyone else but you. Nobody knows me like you.

To Heal

Do you heal by erasing all signs and memories of togetherness? But how do you forget the sensation one has left without a touch?

Do you heal by deleting all potential interactions and chances of reconnecting? But where do we draw the line between growing up and game playing?

Do you heal by holding on to all physical objects and photographs as reminders? But what do we do with a photographic memory related to someone so significant?

If only the hurt you caused could heal like a physical wound that bleeds and the self could heal like a minor burn or a paper cut rather than a wound so deep that it cuts through the nerves and bone that even when the wound is healed, you get a lifelong phantom pain.

Torture

Every time I revisit a memory of our past and of what happened between the period you left until now, it is like self-harm. Why else would one deliberately torture oneself in the hope that the pain will cut through the pain?

I can only hope that patience brings in a realisation that only water can calm a fire when the fuel of your memories runs out.

Photographs

One day, I will take out captured moments from the pages in between the books and in albums. Then place them in direct sunlight and hope that they will fade away in time just like our relationship . . . just like you . . . just like me.

Identity

Never lose yourself to someone or play a role that you lose your identity to. Or you will never find yourself within your own mind, body, and soul.

Call It Quits

At what point do you call it quits? And do I have to call it quits? Why can't I hold on to my pain, my sorrow, my root cause to remission to being in love with someone that meant everything to me? I guess, maybe because he quit on me.

Coffee Stains

That stain on the white T-shirt on a date
    That stain on a notebook whilst journaling
    That stain on the desk whilst revising for an exam
    That stain on a page whilst reading late at night
    That stain on the sofa of a kiss and a cuddle
    Like coffee stains, some will wash away and some will ruin you.
    Yet you can take comfort in the fact that each will fade. . . causing relief of joy or sadness in its fading.

One Last Time

One last call, text, coffee, drink, and night Then say "it's over" for the last time.

On the Same Page

Communicate at every step.

> Otherwise, you may be reading the same book and even be on the same chapter. However, you can be on page 95 whilst the other is on page 5.

FFS Why?

𝓑ut it just doesn't make any sense!

You coming into my life, you leaving and returning into my life!

Or is the answer really so simple and I am looking for a complicated answer to justify your decision and my acceptance?

Worlds Apart

Somehow, we started the journey together, and here we are, at a different destination. Did you lose me, or did I lose you along the way?

Best Bet

Do I want to be your option or choice?

Maybe I want to be your only desire that gives me the option of being a choice.

Strategy

Do I use deception, or do I follow the rules?

Do I use the same tactics you bestowed on me?

I try but can't follow it through, nor can I find the righteous path for victory. However, even unanswered prayers don't let my thoughts waver.

Fidelity

I admire your fidelity to your commitments. But at what expense and why?

Forgiveness

I don't have the capacity to forgive anymore. Does this mean my heart has lost the righteousness that resided within? I sure as hell hope not, because I am most certain forgiving is going to be a lot easier than forgetting.

Partnership

I want to be his inspiration, not his limitation. I want him to be my pride, not my restriction.

Personal Development

Every day is an opportunity to give to the present and a chance to let go of the past.

Every action will be a result of one's character, so refine your character to the best of your ability, with dedication, determination, and devotion.

And every action will have an edge like no other.

Body

It responds to both love and hate. So, screen and test screen what you expose it to. For it might be love that disappoints you the most.

Lifeline

Measure it in moments of peace or regret.

Social Events

Unless it benefits your mind, body, or soul. Unless it gives you hope, confirms your faith, and teaches you to be patient effortlessly.

Sometimes it's best to just send your best wishes rather than attend.

Reasons

I look for a reason to forfeit the hope of your arrival.

I only hope I can find it before I find the reason for your departure.

Otherwise, I'll never find the answers to my whys.

Shelved

You shelved our relationship like an unfinished movie.

I was the raw, conservational art movie you left to make a blockbuster with an upcoming actress with the good fortune of nepotism.

Forgotten in your movie and lost in my script.

However, the script still has a chance of success. Yet you want to remake a failed movie, over and over again.

Complete the Cycle

Follow through your plans with faith.
  Use your hopes as support.
  Don't let the doubts cloud your journey. Have patience, for they are only temporary.

Merger

A merger of love, passion, compassion, and lust is a rare find. Rare find but not impossible.

Blueprint

We can't change our fate, but we can rewrite over it and decide who imprints on it.

Value

I thought you were gold. You turned out to be zinc—in character and in value.

Discover

Discover yourself first, then seek to discover in others. Don't be afraid to take risks, or things will always remain static whilst the world moves on.

Refine

Perhaps the route to an awakening is a refinement of the following:

1. Prayers or good deeds
2. Focus
3. Thoughts

I believe the soul doesn't need refining; it will always be pure for it belongs to the Divine. Untouched and unbiased.

So, let the soul guide the process. Trust it.

Patience within Patience

Have you ever asked yourself "why" or "what you are waiting for" or "the definition of patience?" Are your expectations of the situation or person too great, and if so, do you wait patiently for the situation or person to reach those expectations or lower your own expectations, or just give up completely and lose your patience?

One More, Just One More!

You promised to change. I'm frustrated. One more, just one more!

When is one more one too many?
I can't simply wait no more. I'm tired to the core.
Days become weeks
Weeks become months
How long to hang on? My patience is gone.
The pain of staying
Is stronger than the pain of leaving
Can't take no more
My brain is seething.
The thread of my patience broken in two
One more, just one more because of YOU.

Destruction

They just want it to be quiet

    Boom, boom, boom, sirens all day long

    Saying goodbye is hard, out of sight

    Blowing up bridges, desecrating hospitals, civilians attacked cities and feelings out of whack.

    Black ash and smoking air

    They cannot believe it; we can't let this happen

    They will never give up

    The whole of a society being wiped away.

    Afraid of every sound hands over ears, darkness, shaking and tearful, full of fear at every pound feeling like their drowning in muddy waters, tainted by the smell of death, Perilous mission to defend, children thinking it's all pretend "For one in four of us, every day is a fight," a soldier states. Every day while he is losing his mates.

    Hell on earth, the perfect storm of negative forces,

    A tsunami of war

    Civilians fleeing like galloping horses

Time

I washed you when you were born, my son
    We walked through life together for a time, my son
    Now time has been taken away from you, my son
    My time with you has been taken from me, my son
    I wash you after you died, my son

Mind

My mind bubbling with why me? Why me?
  If only I could see
  My mind confused and at disarray
  Electric wires fused together, trying to find a way
  Who am I, where am I, and what am I?
  Alone and isolated
  People telling you you've deteriorated
  Who am I, where am I, what am I?
  Today's world is online, and if you're not online, the world becomes a much smaller place, socially, environmentally, and even physically (dating).

With Patience

I have the capacity to accept or tolerate delay,
> The patience to sift through the rubbish in my life through the day
>
> I don't have the capacity to accept or tolerate delay
>
> Or the patience to sift through the rubbish today
>
> I deal with problems or suffering without becoming annoyed I don't deal with problems or suffering. I simply destroy
>
> I'm confident in the things I try, I have forbearance at my side
>
> I'm not confident in the things I do, even though I truly tried
>
> I love the challenges that life can bring
>
> Even if the challenge is waiting still
>
> I loathe the challenges that life can bring
>
> I simply am suffering
>
> My will is determined, my mind is clear, not simply under necessity
>
> My will has been burnt, my mind is fog
>
> I have really just had to let it be

Why?

Why did you do that?
>A young man with a full life ahead of him
>Why would you do that? I said
>A handsome man with parents that loved him
>No money worries, a university degree
>However, the light in his life was described as dim
>The pain on his face was there plain to see. The why shouldn't concern me, he said
>There is no why, there just is as he lay there bleeding all over the bed
>Sometimes there is no reason or reasoning
>Like the weather in seasoning
>Sometimes there is no answer right or wrong
>Like the lyrics of a song
>You can't change the now time being dismissed
>Like memories of the first time you kissed
>Life is a mystery that cannot be solved
>You ask yourself why
>The answer is you just have to evolve
>You don't want to live, you can't find your way
>The pain too great to walk through another day

He Who Asks Receives

All you can hear is the telephone ring
    Waiting patiently for what they will bring
    Either an adult, a child, or a baby on the way
    This is how it goes on an average A&E day
    White walls and conversation all around,
    While concentrating on every sound
    Alarms and screams all mixed into one
    At the end of the day, the work is never, ever done.

    Patients on trolleys in discomfort and pain
    Doctors and nurses attending to them again and again
    Medication and treatments offered for relief To try and help them and stop their grief.
    Blood and vomit have dyed the sheets red
    Cuts and bruises on the body and head
    Filling some people with fear and dread
    Some not surviving and being pronounced dead.
    Hospitals being a place of help, a place full of hope, faith, and patience in abode
    Whether struggling with addictions to alcohol or dope
    Or simply just slipped on a bar of soap.
    A place of help for those with mental health illness
    A place full of hope, faith, and patience, nothing less
    A wealth of exceptional knowledge expressed
    Once the nurses and doctors have seen you and assessed.

But sadly also a place of rest, trauma, or cardiac arrest
Nurses and doctors all trying their best; hope and faith lost, nevertheless.

A crazy world in a world often not told
As red tape and policies behold
Only those who work within this world
Have many a story to unfold.

Purpose

*W*hy? (Sometimes there is no why, there just is.)

Authors

*Photography by Kam Vaghela
(Leicester, UK)*

Reena Patel (Leicester, UK)
BSc (Hons) Adult Nursing graduate from De Montfort University Leicester (2004) Nurse of The Year (2017) GP Awards (National)

First generation UK born to parents and grandparents immigrated from India in the '60s to the UK. British Indian woman that has created her own identity and presence within her field of work and roles. Freelance writer for medical and nursing journals/papers. Dog mother of 1 "Sunny" and the best dog aunty to 'Gizmo' Podcaster, and an advocate for physical, emotional, and spiritual well-being, which is reflected in her active social media Instagram page @reena.health

Natalie Hough (Loughborough, UK)
BSc (Hons) Adult Nursing graduate from De Montfort University Leicester (2004)
Ex Accident & Emergency Nurse
Mother of 2,
An inspiration to those who wish to start or change a career at a later point in life. She is a mark of bravery, who went to university at the age of 37 and, as a single parent of 2, Hannah and Santino, successfully established a new start to life. Even after the unfortunate event of having to leave the nursing profession due to ill-health retirement, she was able to accomplish a dream of inspiring others through this book today.

Printed in Great Britain
by Amazon